PUBLICATIONS INTERNATIONAL, LTD.

*Favorite All Time Recipes* is a trademark of Publications International, Ltd.

**Recipe Development:** Beryl Block, Elizabeth King, Laurie Klein and Mary Jane Laws.

Front cover photography and photography on pages 17, 29, 33, 35, 47, 61, 71, 77 and 83 by Sacco Productions Limited, Chicago.

**Pictured on the front cover** *(clockwise from top left)*: Cranberry Raisin Nut Bread *(page 22)*, Cranberry-Orange Relish *(page 30)*, Christmas Citrus Marmalade *(page 31)*, Freezer Plum Conserve *(page 28)*, Carrot & Coriander Soup *(page 12)*, Raspberry Vinegar *(page 34)*, Herbed Vinegar *(page 34)*, Country Pecan Pie *(page 76)*, Holiday Sugar Cookies *(page 44)*, Gingerbread People *(page 43)*, Almond Crescents *(page 54)* and Pecan Cheese Ball *(page 6)*.

**Pictured on the back cover** *(clockwise from top right)*: Chocolate Cream-Filled Cake Roll *(page 82)*, Dark Chocolate Fudge and Peanut Butter Fudge *(page 73)*, Traditional Peanut Brittle *(page 74)*, Chocolate Raspberry Thumbprints *(page 46)* and Elephant Ears *(page 46)*.

ISBN: 0-7853-0707-9

Manufactured in U.S.A.

8  7  6  5  4  3  2  1

Microwave ovens vary in wattage. The microwave cooking times given in this publication are approximate. Use the cooking times as guidelines and check for doneness before adding more time.

Country Christmas RECIPES

# Seasonal Starters

## PECAN CHEESE BALL

  1 package (8 ounces) cream cheese, softened
¼ cup finely chopped parsley
  2 tablespoons finely chopped chives
½ teaspoon Worcestershire sauce
    Dash hot pepper sauce
¾ cup finely chopped pecans
    Assorted crackers

Combine all ingredients except pecans and crackers in medium bowl. Cover; refrigerate until firm. Form cheese mixture into a ball. Roll in pecans. Store tightly wrapped in plastic wrap in refrigerator. Allow cheese ball to soften at room temperature before serving with crackers. *Makes one cheese ball*

**Gift Tip:** Give Pecan Cheese Ball with an assortment of other cheeses, a wooden cheese board, a jar of imported pickles or mustard and/or a bag of pecans.

**Variations:** Form cheese mixture into 1½-inch balls. Roll in paprika, chopped herbs, such as parsley, watercress or basil, or chopped green olives instead of pecans.

*Top to bottom: Pecan Cheese Ball (variations) and Cheddar Cheese Spread (page 12)*

# CREAMY CUCUMBER-YOGURT DIP

1 cucumber
Salt
¼ cup chopped chives, divided
1 package (8 ounces) cream cheese, softened
¼ cup plain yogurt
1 tablespoon fresh lemon juice
1½ teaspoons dried mint leaves, crushed
Freshly ground black pepper
Assorted cut-up vegetables

Peel cucumber; cut in half lengthwise. Scoop out seeds with teaspoon; discard. Finely chop cucumber. Lightly salt cucumber in small bowl; toss. Refrigerate 1 hour. Drain cucumber; dry on paper towels. Set aside.

Reserve 1 tablespoon chives for garnish. Place remaining 3 tablespoons chives, cream cheese, yogurt, lemon juice, mint and pepper in food processor or blender; process until smooth. Place cheese mixture in bowl. Stir in cucumber. Cover; refrigerate 1 hour. Spoon dip into glass bowl or gift container; sprinkle reserved chives over top. Cover and store up to 2 days in refrigerator. Stir before serving with vegetables.

*Makes about 2 cups dip*

# SPICY COCKTAIL SAUCE

1 cup tomato ketchup
2 cloves garlic, finely chopped
1 tablespoon fresh lemon juice
1 teaspoon prepared horseradish
¾ teaspoon chili powder
½ teaspoon salt
¼ teaspoon hot pepper sauce *or* ⅛ teaspoon ground
   red pepper (cayenne)

Combine all ingredients in medium bowl; blend well. Spoon into glass bowl and serve with cooked seafood *or* pour into clean glass jar and seal tightly. Store up to 1 year in refrigerator.

*Makes 1⅓ cups sauce, enough for 1 pound of seafood*

**Gift Tip:** If you are giving this to someone who lives nearby, it would be a charming thought to present it with some fresh chilled cooked shrimp.

*Creamy Cucumber-Yogurt Dip (top) and*
*Spicy Cocktail Sauce (bottom)*

# RED BEAN SOUP

1 pound dried red kidney beans
1 sprig thyme
1 sprig parsley
2 tablespoons butter or margarine
1 small onion, finely chopped
4 carrots, peeled and chopped
2 ribs celery, chopped
1½ quarts water
1 pound smoked ham hocks
1 bay leaf
3 cloves garlic, finely chopped
½ teaspoon salt
¼ teaspoon pepper
2 tablespoons fresh lemon juice
   Dairy sour cream, for garnish
   "Holly" leaf and berry cutouts, made from green and red bell
     peppers (optional)

Soak beans in 1 quart water in large bowl 6 hours or overnight. Drain, rinse and set aside. Tie together thyme and parsley sprigs with thread; set aside.

Heat butter in heavy, large stockpot over medium-high heat until melted and bubbly. Cook and stir onion in hot butter 3 minutes or until onion is softened. Add carrots and celery; cook and stir 5 minutes or until browned. Add 1½ quarts water, beans, ham, bay leaf, garlic and reserved thyme and parsley sprigs. Bring to a boil over high heat. Reduce heat to low. Cover; simmer 1¼ to 1½ hours until beans are softened. Discard bones, thyme and parsley sprigs and bay leaf. Stir in salt and pepper.

Process soup in batches in food processor or blender until smooth. Return to saucepan. Heat to simmering; stir in lemon juice and season to taste. Ladle into bowls. Garnish with dollops of sour cream and green pepper "leaves" and red pepper "berries," if desired.    *Makes 6 servings*

**Gift Tip:** Give this soup in an attractive glass jar accompanied by soup bowls. Store up to 1 week in refrigerator. Reheat before serving.

**Black Bean Soup:** Substitute black beans for the red kidney beans. Proceed as directed, simmering soup 1½ to 2 hours or until beans are tender. Add 4 to 5 tablespoons sherry, to taste, just before serving.

**Cranberry Bean Soup:** Substitute cranberry beans for the red kidney beans. Proceed as directed, simmering soup 2 to 2¼ hours or until beans are tender. (Cranberry beans can be found in specialty food stores. They are the color of cranberries but taste similar to kidney beans. Give soup with an extra box of cranberry beans for a gift idea. These beans are great in salads.)

*Top to bottom: Carrot & Coriander Soup*
*(page 12) and Red Bean Soup*

# CHEDDAR CHEESE SPREAD

3 ounces *each* white Cheddar, yellow Cheddar and cream cheese, cut
    into small pieces
6 green onions, white parts only, finely chopped
2 tablespoons butter or margarine, softened
2 tablespoons dry sherry
1 teaspoon Worcestershire sauce
1 teaspoon Dijon-style mustard
¼ teaspoon salt (optional)
    Dash hot pepper sauce (optional)
2 tablespoons finely chopped chives
    Assorted crackers

Place all ingredients except chives and crackers in food processor or blender;
process until smooth. Add chives; pulse to mix in. Place in crock or gift
container. Cover; refrigerate. Allow spread to soften at room temperature
before serving. Serve with crackers.     *Makes about 2 cups spread*

**Gift Tip:** Include a box of crackers with the crock of spread.

# CARROT & CORIANDER SOUP

4 tablespoons butter or margarine
4 cups grated carrots (about 1 pound)
1 cup finely chopped onion
3 cups chicken broth
2 tablespoons fresh lemon juice
1½ teaspoons ground coriander
1½ teaspoons ground cumin
1 clove garlic, finely chopped
2 tablespoons finely chopped fresh coriander (cilantro)
    Salt and pepper

Heat butter in medium saucepan over medium-high heat until melted and
bubbly. Cook and stir carrots and onion in hot butter 5 minutes or until
onions begin to soften. Add broth, lemon juice, ground coriander, cumin and
garlic. Bring to a boil over high heat. Reduce heat to low. Cover; simmer 25 to
30 minutes until vegetables are soft.

Process soup in batches in food processor or blender until smooth. Stir in
fresh coriander. Season to taste. Serve immediately *or* cool and pour into clean
glass jars; seal tightly. Store up to 1 week in refrigerator. Reheat before
serving.     *Makes 4 to 6 servings*

# CHEESE TWISTS

> 1 cup all-purpose flour
> ½ teaspoon baking soda
> ½ teaspoon dry mustard
> ½ teaspoon salt
> ⅛ teaspoon ground red pepper (cayenne)
> ¾ cup grated Parmesan cheese, divided
> ½ cup butter or margarine, softened
> 3 egg yolks
> 2 teaspoons water
> 1 egg white, slightly beaten
> 1 tablespoon sesame seeds (optional)

Preheat oven to 400°F. Grease two cookie sheets. Combine flour, baking soda, mustard, salt and red pepper in large bowl. Reserve 1 tablespoon cheese; stir remaining cheese into flour mixture. Cut in butter with pastry blender or 2 knives until mixture resembles fine crumbs. Add egg yolks and water, mixing until dough forms. Shape into a ball; flatten and wrap in plastic wrap. Refrigerate 2 hours or until firm.

Roll out dough on lightly floured surface into 12-inch square (about ⅛ inch thick). Brush surface lightly with egg white and sprinkle with remaining 1 tablespoon cheese and sesame seeds, if desired. Cut dough in half. Cut each half crosswise into ¼-inch strips. Twist 2 strips together. Repeat with remaining strips. Place 1 inch apart on prepared cookie sheets.

Bake 6 to 8 minutes until light golden brown. Remove from cookie sheets and cool completely on wire racks. Store in airtight container.

*Makes about 48 twists*

**Variation:** Prepare dough and cut as directed. Place ¾ of strips on cookie sheets. Form rings with remaining strips; seal edges. Place on cookie sheets. Bake and cool as directed. To serve, arrange 3 to 4 strips into small stacks. Insert stacks into rings.

# DEVILED MIXED NUTS

3 tablespoons vegetable oil
2 cups assorted unsalted nuts, such as peanuts, almonds,
　　Brazil nuts or walnuts
2 tablespoons sugar
1 teaspoon paprika
½ teaspoon ground chili powder
½ teaspoon curry powder
½ teaspoon ground cumin
½ teaspoon ground coriander
½ teaspoon ground black pepper
¼ teaspoon salt

Heat oil in large skillet over medium heat; cook and stir nuts in hot oil 2 to
3 minutes until browned. Combine remaining ingredients in small bowl;
sprinkle over nuts. Stir to coat evenly. Heat 1 to 2 minutes more. Drain nuts
on wire rack lined with paper towels. Serve warm.

*Makes 6 to 8 servings or 2 cups nuts*

# MARINATED MUSHROOMS

1 pint uniformly sized small white button mushroom caps,
　　washed and left whole
½ cup olive oil
3 tablespoons tarragon vinegar
¼ cup finely chopped parsley
1 tablespoon Dijon-style mustard
3 cloves garlic, finely chopped
1 teaspoon sugar
¾ teaspoon dried tarragon leaves, crushed
½ teaspoon salt
　Freshly ground black pepper to taste

Fill 16-ounce jar with mushrooms, arranging attractively. Process remaining
ingredients in food processor or combine in small bowl with wire whisk.
Pour dressing into jar to cover mushrooms completely. Seal jar and marinate
overnight to blend flavors. Store up to 1 week in refrigerator.

*Makes about 6 servings or 3 cups mushrooms*

*Top to bottom: Cheese Twists (page 13)
and Deviled Mixed Nuts*

# Yuletide Breads

## CHERRY EGGNOG QUICK BREAD

2½ cups all-purpose flour
¾ cup sugar
1 tablespoon baking powder
½ teaspoon ground nutmeg
1¼ cups prepared dairy eggnog
6 tablespoons butter or margarine, melted
2 eggs, slightly beaten
1 teaspoon vanilla extract
½ cup chopped pecans
½ cup chopped candied red cherries

Preheat oven to 350°F. Grease 9×5-inch loaf pan.*

Combine flour, sugar, baking powder and nutmeg in large bowl. Stir eggnog, melted butter, eggs and vanilla in medium bowl until well blended. Add eggnog mixture to flour mixture. Mix just until all ingredients are moistened. Stir in pecans and cherries. Spoon into prepared pan.

Bake 45 to 50 minutes until wooden pick inserted in center comes out clean. Cool in pan 15 minutes. Remove from pan and cool completely on wire rack. Store tightly wrapped in plastic wrap at room temperature.

*Makes one 9×5-inch loaf*

*Bread may also be baked in three 5½×3-inch greased mini-loaf pans. Prepare batter as directed. Bake at 350°F for 35 to 40 minutes until wooden pick inserted in center comes out clean. Proceed as directed.

*Cherry Eggnog Quick Bread*

# WHOLE WHEAT HERBED BREAD WREATH

    4 cups all-purpose flour, divided
    2 packages active dry yeast
    2 tablespoons sugar
    4 teaspoons dried rosemary leaves, crushed
    1 tablespoon salt
2½ cups water
    2 tablespoons olive oil
    3 cups whole wheat flour, divided
    1 egg, beaten

Combine 2½ cups all-purpose flour, yeast, sugar, rosemary and salt in large bowl. Heat water until very warm (120° to 130°F). Gradually add to flour mixture with oil until blended. Beat with electric mixer on medium speed 2 minutes. Add 1 cup whole wheat flour. Beat on high speed 2 minutes, scraping sides of bowl occasionally. By hand, stir in enough of remaining flours to make a soft, sticky dough. Place in greased bowl; turn to grease top of dough. Cover with towel. Let rise in warm, draft-free place about 1½ hours or until double in volume.

Punch dough down. Turn out onto well-floured surface. Knead about 10 minutes or until smooth and elastic. Divide into thirds. Roll each piece to form 24-inch rope. Place on large greased cookie sheet. Braid ropes beginning at center and working toward ends. Seal edges. Shape into circle around greased 10-ounce *ovenproof* round bowl. Seal ends well. Cover with towel. Let rise in warm, draft-free place about 30 minutes or until double in volume.

Preheat oven to 450°F. Carefully brush wreath with egg. Bake 25 to 30 minutes until wreath sounds hollow when tapped and top is golden brown. Cool on cookie sheet 10 minutes. Carefully remove from cookie sheet and bowl; cool completely on wire rack. Store tightly wrapped in plastic wrap at room temperature.

*Makes one 12-inch wreath*

*Whole Wheat Herbed Bread Wreath*

# SPICY GINGERBREAD WITH CINNAMON PEAR SAUCE

    2 cups all-purpose flour
 ½ cup packed light brown sugar
    1 teaspoon baking soda
    1 teaspoon ground ginger
    1 teaspoon ground cinnamon
 ¼ teaspoon ground cloves
 ¼ teaspoon salt
    1 cup light molasses
 ¾ cup buttermilk
 ½ cup butter or margarine, softened
    Cinnamon Pear Sauce (recipe follows)

Preheat oven to 325°F. Grease and lightly flour 9-inch square baking pan.

Combine all ingredients except Cinnamon Pear Sauce in large bowl. Beat with electric mixer on low speed until well blended, scraping sides of bowl with rubber spatula frequently. Beat on high speed 2 minutes more. Pour into prepared pan.

Bake 50 to 55 minutes until wooden pick inserted in center comes out clean. Cool in pan on wire rack about 30 minutes. Cut into squares; serve warm with Cinnamon Pear Sauce.
*Makes 9 servings*

## Cinnamon Pear Sauce

    2 cans (16 ounces each) pear halves in syrup, undrained
    2 tablespoons granulated sugar
    1 teaspoon fresh lemon juice
 ½ teaspoon ground cinnamon

Drain pear halves, reserving ¼ cup syrup. Place pears, reserved syrup, granulated sugar, lemon juice and cinnamon in work bowl of food processor or blender; cover. Process until smooth. Just before serving, place pear sauce in medium saucepan; heat until warm.
*Makes 2 cups sauce*

# TOMATO AND CHEESE FOCACCIA

1 package active dry yeast
¾ cup warm water (105° to 115°F)
2 cups all-purpose flour
½ teaspoon salt
¼ cup olive oil, divided
1 teaspoon Italian seasoning
8 oil-packed sun-dried tomatoes, well drained
½ cup (2 ounces) shredded provolone cheese
¼ cup (1 ounce) freshly grated Parmesan cheese

Dissolve yeast in warm water; let stand 5 minutes. Combine flour and salt in work bowl of food processor.* Stir in yeast mixture and 3 tablespoons oil. Process until ingredients form a ball. Process 1 minute more. Turn out onto lightly floured surface. Knead about 2 minutes or until smooth and elastic. Place dough in oiled bowl; turn to oil top of dough. Cover with towel. Let rise in warm, draft-free place about 30 minutes or until double in volume.

Punch dough down. Let rest 5 minutes. Press dough into oiled 10-inch cake pan, deep-dish pizza pan or springform pan. Brush with remaining 1 tablespoon oil. Sprinkle with Italian seasoning. Press sun-dried tomatoes around side of pan, about 1 inch from edge. Sprinkle with cheeses. Cover with towel. Let rise in warm, draft-free place 15 minutes.

Preheat oven to 425°F. Bake 20 to 25 minutes until golden brown. Cool completely in pan on wire rack. Carefully remove side and bottom of pan before serving. *Makes one 10-inch bread*

*If mixing dough by hand, combine flour and salt in large bowl. Stir in yeast mixture and 3 tablespoons oil until ingredients form a ball. Turn out onto lightly floured surface and knead about 10 minutes or until smooth and elastic. Proceed as directed.

# CRANBERRY RAISIN NUT BREAD

1½ cups all-purpose flour
¾ cup packed light brown sugar
1½ teaspoons baking powder
½ teaspoon baking soda
½ teaspoon ground cinnamon
½ teaspoon ground nutmeg
1 cup halved fresh or frozen cranberries
½ cup golden raisins
½ cup coarsely chopped pecans
1 tablespoon grated orange peel
2 eggs
¾ cup milk
3 tablespoons butter or margarine, melted
1 teaspoon vanilla extract
Cranberry-Orange Spread (recipe follows), optional

Preheat oven to 350°F. Grease 8½ × 4½-inch loaf pan.

Combine flour, brown sugar, baking powder, baking soda, cinnamon and nutmeg in large bowl. Stir in cranberries, raisins, pecans and orange peel. Mix eggs, milk, melted butter and vanilla in small bowl until combined; stir into flour mixture just until moistened. Spoon into prepared pan.

Bake 55 to 60 minutes until wooden pick inserted in center comes out clean. Cool in pan 15 minutes. Remove from pan and cool completely on wire rack. Store tightly wrapped in plastic wrap at room temperature. Serve slices with Cranberry-Orange Spread, if desired.          *Makes one 8½ × 4½-inch loaf*

# Cranberry-Orange Spread

1 package (8 ounces) cream cheese, softened
1 package (3 ounces) cream cheese, softened
1 container (12 ounces) cranberry-orange sauce
¾ cup chopped pecans

Combine cream cheese and cranberry-orange sauce in small bowl. Stir with spoon until blended. Stir in pecans. Store refrigerated.

*Makes about 3 cups spread*

*Cranberry Raisin Nut Bread*

# HOLIDAY PUMPKIN-NUT MUFFINS

2½ cups all-purpose flour
  1 cup packed light brown sugar
  1 tablespoon baking powder
  1 teaspoon ground cinnamon
½ teaspoon ground nutmeg
½ teaspoon ground ginger
¼ teaspoon salt
  1 cup canned pumpkin (not pumpkin pie filling)
¾ cup milk
  2 eggs
  6 tablespoons butter or margarine, melted
⅔ cup roasted, salted pepitas (pumpkin seeds), divided
½ cup golden raisins

Preheat oven to 400°F. Grease or paper-line 18 (2¾-inch) muffin cups.

Combine flour, brown sugar, baking powder, cinnamon, nutmeg, ginger and salt in large bowl. Stir pumpkin, milk, eggs and melted butter in medium bowl until well blended. Stir pumpkin mixture into flour mixture. Mix *just* until all ingredients are moistened. Stir in ⅓ cup pepitas and raisins. Spoon into prepared muffin cups, filling ⅔ full. Sprinkle remaining pepitas over muffin batter.

Bake 15 to 18 minutes until wooden pick inserted in center comes out clean. Cool in pans 10 minutes. Remove from pans and cool completely on wire racks. Store in airtight container.     *Makes 18 (2¾-inch) muffins*

*Holiday Pumpkin-Nut Muffins*

# FESTIVE YULE LOAF

2¾ cups all-purpose flour, divided
⅓ cup sugar
1 teaspoon salt
1 package active dry yeast
1 cup milk
½ cup butter or margarine
1 egg
½ cup golden raisins
½ cup chopped candied red and green cherries
½ cup chopped pecans
  Vanilla Glaze (recipe follows), optional

Combine 1½ cups flour, sugar, salt and yeast in large bowl. Heat milk and butter over medium heat until very warm (120° to 130°F). Gradually stir into flour mixture. Add egg. Mix with electric mixer on low speed 1 minute. Beat on high speed 3 minutes, scraping sides of bowl frequently. Toss raisins, cherries and pecans with ¼ cup flour in small bowl; stir into yeast mixture. Stir in enough of remaining 1 cup flour to make a soft dough. Turn out onto lightly floured surface. Knead about 10 minutes or until smooth and elastic. Place in greased bowl; turn to grease top of dough. Cover with towel. Let rise in warm, draft-free place about 1 hour or until double in volume.

Punch dough down. Divide in half. Roll out each half on lightly floured surface to form 8-inch circle. Fold in half; press only folded edge firmly. Place on ungreased cookie sheet. Cover with towel. Let rise in warm, draft-free place about 30 minutes or until double in volume.

Preheat oven to 375°F. Bake 20 to 25 minutes until golden brown. Remove from cookie sheet and cool completely on wire rack. Frost with Vanilla Glaze, if desired. Store in airtight containers.                    *Makes 2 loaves*

*Vanilla Glaze:* Combine 1 cup sifted powdered sugar, 4 to 5 teaspoons light cream or half-and-half and ½ teaspoon vanilla extract in small bowl; stir until smooth.

# SPICY MINCEMEAT BREAD

  6 tablespoons butter or margarine
  1 cup packed light brown sugar
  2 eggs
  1 teaspoon vanilla extract
2½ cups all-purpose flour
1½ teaspoons baking soda
  1 teaspoon ground cinnamon
  ¾ teaspoon baking powder
  ½ teaspoon ground nutmeg
  ¼ teaspoon salt
  ¾ cup dairy sour cream
  1 cup prepared mincemeat
  ¾ cup chopped pecans

Preheat oven to 350°F. Grease 9×5-inch loaf pan.*

Beat butter and brown sugar in large bowl with electric mixer on medium speed until light and fluffy. Beat in eggs and vanilla until blended. Combine flour, baking soda, cinnamon, baking powder, nutmeg and salt. Add flour mixture to butter mixture on low speed alternately with sour cream, beginning and ending with flour mixture. Mix well after each addition. Stir in mincemeat and pecans on low speed until blended. Spoon into prepared pan.

Bake 55 to 60 minutes until wooden pick inserted in center comes out clean. Cool in pan 15 minutes. Remove from pan and cool completely on wire rack. Store tightly wrapped in plastic wrap at room temperature.

*Makes one 9×5-inch loaf*

*Bread may also be baked in four 5½×3-inch greased mini-loaf pans. Prepare batter as directed. Bake at 350°F for 45 to 50 minutes until wooden pick inserted in center comes out clean. Proceed as directed.

# Gifts in a Jar

## FREEZER PLUM CONSERVE

4 (½-pint) jelly jars with lids
2 cans (16 ounces each) whole purple plums, drained and pitted
1 tablespoon grated orange peel
1 large orange, peeled and sectioned
4 cups sugar
1 cup raisins
½ cup chopped walnuts
¾ cup water
1 box (1¾ ounces) powdered fruit pectin

Rinse clean jars and lids with boiling water.

Place plums, orange peel and orange sections in food processor or blender. Process until plums are chopped. Measure 2 cups mixture into large bowl.

Stir sugar into plum mixture. Stir until well blended. Stir in raisins and walnuts. Let stand for 10 minutes, stirring occasionally.

Mix water and pectin in 1-quart saucepan. (Mixture may be lumpy.) Bring to a boil over high heat, stirring constantly. Boil and stir 1 minute. Stir hot pectin mixture into fruit mixture. Stir constantly for 3 minutes.

Ladle hot mixture into jars leaving ½-inch space at top. Run metal spatula around inside of jar to remove air bubbles. Wipe tops and sides of jar rims clean; quickly cover with lids. Let stand at room temperature up to 24 hours or until set. Store in freezer up to 12 months. Thaw jars in refrigerator overnight before using. Refrigerate after opening up to 6 months.

*Makes about four ½-pint jars*

*Clockwise from top: Cranberry-Orange Relish (page 30), Christmas Citrus Marmalade (page 31) and Freezer Plum Conserve*

# CRANBERRY-ORANGE RELISH

4 large oranges, divided
7 (½-pint) jelly jars with lids and screw bands
2 cups sugar
½ cup water
2 packages (12 ounces each) fresh cranberries, washed and drained

Remove peel from white part of 2 oranges in long strips with sharp paring knife, making sure there is no white on the peel. Stack strips; cut into thin slivers. Measure ¼ cup.

Add orange peel to 1 inch boiling water in 1-quart saucepan. Boil over medium heat 5 minutes. Drain and set aside. Peel remaining 2 oranges and remove white pith from all 4 oranges; discard peel and pith. Separate oranges into sections. With fingers, remove pulp from membrane of each section over 2-cup measure to save juice. Dice orange sections into same cup measure. Add additional water to orange mixture to make 2 cups, if necessary.

Wash jars, lids and bands. Leave jars in hot water. Place lids and bands in large pan of water.

Combine sugar and water in heavy 6-quart saucepan or Dutch oven. Bring to a boil over medium heat. Add reserved orange peel, orange mixture and cranberries. Bring to a boil, stirring occasionally. Boil about 10 minutes or until mixture thickens gently and cranberries pop.

Bring water with lids and bands to a boil. Ladle hot mixture into hot jars leaving ½-inch space at top. Run metal spatula around inside of jar to remove air bubbles. Wipe tops and sides of jar rims clean. Place hot lids and bands on jar. Screw bands tightly, but do not force. To process, place jars in boiling water; boil 10 minutes. Remove jars with tongs; cool on wire racks. (Check seals by pressing on lid with fingertip; lid should remain concave.) Label and date jars. Store unopened jars in a cool, dry place up to 12 months. Refrigerate after opening up to 6 months. *Makes about seven ½-pint jars*

# RICH CHOCOLATE SAUCE

1 cup whipping cream
⅓ cup light corn syrup
1 cup (6 ounces) semisweet chocolate chips
1 to 2 tablespoons dark rum (optional)
1 teaspoon vanilla extract

*(continued)*

Place cream and corn syrup in heavy 2-quart saucepan. Stir over medium heat until mixture boils. Remove from heat. Stir in chocolate, rum, if desired, and vanilla until chocolate is melted. Cool 10 minutes. Serve warm or pour into clean glass jars and seal tightly. Store up to 6 months in refrigerator. Reheat sauce over low heat before serving. *Makes about 1¾ cups sauce*

# CHRISTMAS CITRUS MARMALADE

  2 lemons
  1 orange
2½ cups water
  ⅛ teaspoon baking soda
  1 large grapefruit
  7 (½-pint) jelly jars with lids and screw bands
  1 box (1¾ ounces) powdered fruit pectin
  6 cups sugar

Remove peel from white part of lemons and orange in long strips with sharp paring knife, making sure there is no white on the peel. Stack strips; cut into thin slivers. Combine lemon and orange peels, water and baking soda in 2-quart saucepan. Bring to a boil over high heat. Reduce heat to low; cover and simmer 20 minutes, stirring occasionally.

Meanwhile, peel grapefruit; remove white pith from grapefruit, lemons and orange; discard peel and pith. Separate fruit into sections. With fingers, remove pulp from membrane of each section over large saucepan to save juice. Dice fruit sections into saucepan with lemon and orange peel mixture. Bring to a boil. Cover and simmer 10 minutes. Measure 5 cups fruit mixture into 6-quart saucepan or Dutch oven; discard any remaining mixture.

Wash jars, lids and bands. Leave jars in hot water. Place lids and bands in large pan of water. Mix pectin into fruit mixture. Bring to a rolling boil over medium-high heat, stirring constantly. Immediately stir in sugar. Bring to a rolling boil and boil 1 minute, stirring constantly. Remove from heat; skim off foam with metal spoon.

Bring water with lids and bands to a boil. Ladle hot mixture into hot jars leaving ½-inch space at top. Run metal spatula around inside of jar to remove air bubbles. Wipe tops and sides of jar rims clean. Place hot lids and bands on jar. Screw bands tightly, but do not force. To process, place jars in boiling water; boil 10 minutes. Remove jars with tongs; cool on wire racks. (Check seals by pressing on lid with fingertip; lid should remain concave.) Label and date jars.* Store unopened jars in a cool, dry place up to 12 months. Refrigerate after opening up to 6 months. *Makes about seven ½-pint jars*

*Marmalade sets slowly. Store in a cool, dry place 2 weeks before serving.

# MOCHA COFFEE MIX

1 cup nonfat dry milk powder
¾ cup granulated sugar
⅔ cup powdered non-dairy creamer
½ cup unsweetened cocoa
⅓ cup instant coffee, pressed through fine sieve
¼ cup packed brown sugar
1 teaspoon ground cinnamon
¼ teaspoon salt
¼ teaspoon ground nutmeg

Combine all ingredients in 1-quart airtight container or decorative gift jar; cover. *Makes about 3¼ cups mix or 10 to 12 servings*

**For single serving:** Place rounded ¼ cup Mocha Coffee Mix in mug or cup; add ¾ cup boiling water. Stir until mix is dissolved. Serve immediately.

# EASY COCOA MIX

2 cups nonfat dry milk powder
1 cup sugar
¾ cup powdered non-dairy creamer
½ cup unsweetened cocoa
¼ teaspoon salt

Combine all ingredients in 1-quart airtight container or decorative gift jar; cover. *Makes about 4 cups mix or 16 servings*

**For single serving:** Place rounded ¼ cup Easy Cocoa Mix in mug or cup; add ¾ cup boiling water. Stir until mix is dissolved. Top with sweetened whipped cream and marshmallows, if desired. Serve immediately.

**Cocoa Marshmallow Mix:** Prepare Easy Cocoa Mix in 2-quart airtight container as directed adding 1 package (10½ ounces) miniature marshmallows. *Makes about 7 cups mix or 14 servings*

**For single serving:** Place rounded ½ cup Cocoa Marshmallow Mix in mug or cup; add ¾ cup boiling water. Stir until mix is dissolved. Serve immediately.

*Easy Cocoa Mix (left) and
Mocha Coffee Mix (right)*

# HERBED VINEGAR

**1 bottle (12 ounces) white wine vinegar (1½ cups)**
**½ cup fresh basil leaves**

Pour vinegar into non-aluminum 2-quart saucepan. Heat until very hot, stirring occasionally. *Do not boil.* (If vinegar boils, it will become cloudy.)

Pour into glass bowl; add basil. Cover with plastic wrap. Let stand in cool place about 1 week until desired amount of flavor develops. Strain before using. Store up to 6 months in jar or bottle with tight-fitting lid.

*Makes about 1½ cups vinegar*

**Variations:** Substitute 1 tablespoon of either fresh oregano, thyme, chervil or tarragon for the basil. Or, substitute cider vinegar for the wine vinegar.

# RASPBERRY VINEGAR

**1 bottle (12 ounces) white wine vinegar (1½ cups)**
**½ cup sugar**
**1 cup fresh raspberries or sliced strawberries, crushed**

Combine vinegar and sugar in non-aluminum 2-quart saucepan. Heat until very hot, stirring occasionally. *Do not boil.* (If vinegar boils, it will become cloudy.)

Pour into glass bowl; stir in raspberries. Cover with plastic wrap. Let stand in cool place about 1 week until desired amount of flavor develops. Strain through fine mesh sieve or cheesecloth twice. Store up to 6 months in jar or bottle with tight-fitting lid in refrigerator.          *Makes about 2 cups vinegar*

*Herbed Vinegar (left) and*
*Raspberry Vinegar (right)*

# CREAMY CARAMEL SAUCE

  1 cup granulated sugar
  1 cup whipping cream
  ½ cup packed light brown sugar
  ⅓ cup corn syrup
  1 teaspoon vanilla extract

Place granulated sugar, cream, brown sugar and corn syrup in heavy 2-quart saucepan. Stir over low heat until mixture boils. Carefully clip candy thermometer to side of pan (do not let bulb touch bottom of pan). Cook, stirring occasionally, about 20 minutes or until thermometer registers 238°F. Immediately remove from heat. Stir in vanilla. Cool about 15 minutes. Serve warm or pour into clean glass jars and seal tightly. Store up to 6 months in refrigerator. Reheat sauce over low heat before serving.

*Makes about 2 cups sauce*

# GOOEY HOT FUDGE SAUCE

  2 cups (12 ounces) semisweet chocolate chips
  2 tablespoons butter
  ½ cup half-and-half
  1 tablespoon corn syrup
  ⅛ teaspoon salt
  ½ teaspoon vanilla extract

Melt chocolate and butter with half-and-half, corn syrup and salt in heavy 2-quart saucepan over low heat, stirring until smooth. Remove from heat; let stand 10 minutes. Stir in vanilla. Serve warm or pour into clean glass jars and seal tightly. Store up to 6 months in refrigerator. Reheat sauce in double-boiler over hot (not boiling) water before serving, if desired.

*Makes about 1½ cups sauce*

*Clockwise from top left: Spicy Cocktail Sauce (page 8), Gooey Hot Fudge Sauce, Rich Chocolate Sauce (page 30) and Creamy Caramel Sauce*

# HOLIDAY APPLE CHUTNEY

9 (½-pint) jelly jars with lids and screw bands
8 large tart apples, peeled, cored and chopped (about 4 pounds)
2 large onions, chopped
2 cups golden raisins
1 package (16 ounces) packed brown sugar (2¼ cups)
2 cups granulated sugar
1 cup cider vinegar
   Grated peel and juice of 2 oranges and 1 lemon
2 tablespoons finely chopped crystallized ginger
2 teaspoons ground cinnamon
½ teaspoon ground cloves

Wash jars, lids and bands. Leave jars in hot water. Place lids and bands in large pan of water.

Combine remaining ingredients in heavy 8-quart saucepan or Dutch oven. Bring to a boil over high heat. Reduce heat to medium-low. Simmer, uncovered, 30 minutes or until mixture thickens, stirring frequently.

Bring water with lids and bands to a boil. Ladle hot mixture into hot jars leaving ½-inch space at top. Run metal spatula around inside of jar to remove air bubbles. Wipe tops and sides of jar rims clean. Place hot lids and bands on jar. Screw bands tightly, but do not force. To process, place jars in boiling water; boil 10 minutes. Remove jars with tongs; cool on wire racks. (Check seals by pressing on lid with fingertip; lid should remain concave.) Label and date jars. Store unopened jars in a cool, dry place up to 12 months. Refrigerate after opening up to 6 months. *Makes about nine ½-pint jars*

# CROCK OF SPICE FOR APPLE CIDER

12 cinnamon sticks, broken into small pieces
¼ cup whole cloves
¼ cup allspice berries
¼ cup juniper berries
1 tablespoon dried orange peel, chopped
1 tablespoon dried lemon peel, chopped
1 teaspoon ground nutmeg

*(continued)*

Combine all ingredients in airtight container. To prepare spiced cider, measure 1 heaping teaspoon spice mixture for each mug of cider into large saucepan. Simmer cider with spices for 5 minutes. Strain before serving.

**Gift Tip:** Put mixture in crock or attractive container and give with jug of country apple cider from your favorite farm stand or market. Include above instructions for making spiced cider on a recipe card with the gift.

**Variation:** Pack into small bags you have made from Christmas fabrics or into muslin bouquet garni bags available at kitchen or specialty stores. Use like tea bags to flavor mugs of hot cider or mulled wine.

# SPICY GERMAN MUSTARD

½ **cup mustard seeds**
2 **tablespoons dry mustard**
½ **cup cold water**
1 **cup cider vinegar**
1 **small onion, chopped (about ¼ cup)**
2 **cloves garlic, minced**
3 **tablespoons packed brown sugar**
¾ **teaspoon salt**
¼ **teaspoon dried tarragon leaves, crushed**
¼ **teaspoon ground cinnamon**

Combine mustard seeds, dry mustard and water in small bowl. Cover; let stand at least 4 hours or overnight.

Combine vinegar, onion, garlic, brown sugar, salt, tarragon and cinnamon in non-corrosive heavy 1-quart saucepan. Bring to a boil over high heat; reduce heat to medium. Boil, uncovered, about 7 to 10 minutes until mixture is reduced by half.

Pour vinegar mixture through fine sieve into food processor bowl. Rinse saucepan; set aside. Add mustard mixture to vinegar mixture; process about 1 minute or until mustard seeds are chopped but not puréed. Pour into same saucepan. Cook over low heat until mustard is thick, stirring constantly. Store in airtight container or decorative gift jars up to 1 year in refrigerator.

*Makes about 1 cup*

# Santa's Favorite Cookies

## GOOEY CARAMEL CHOCOLATE BARS

    2 cups all-purpose flour
    1 cup granulated sugar
    ¼ teaspoon salt
    2 cups butter or margarine, divided
    1 cup packed light brown sugar
    ⅓ cup light corn syrup
    1 cup (6 ounces) semisweet chocolate chips

Preheat oven to 350°F. Line 13×9-inch baking pan with foil. Combine flour, granulated sugar and salt in medium bowl; stir until blended. Cut in 14 tablespoons (1¾ sticks) butter until mixture resembles course crumbs. Press into bottom of prepared pan.

Bake 18 to 20 minutes until lightly browned around edges. Remove pan to wire rack; cool completely.

Combine 1 cup butter, brown sugar and corn syrup in heavy medium saucepan. Cook over medium heat 5 to 8 minutes until mixture boils, stirring frequently. Boil gently 2 minutes, without stirring. Immediately pour over cooled base; spread evenly to edges of pan with metal spatula. Cool completely.

Melt chocolate in double boiler over hot (not simmering) water. Stir in remaining 2 tablespoons butter. Pour over cooled caramel layer and spread evenly to edges of pan with metal spatula. Refrigerate 10 to 15 minutes until chocolate begins to set. Remove from refrigerator; cool completely. Cut into bars.
                                                          *Makes 3 dozen bars*

*Top to bottom: Oat-y Nut Bars (page 42)
and Gooey Caramel Chocolate Bars*

# OAT-Y NUT BARS

½ cup butter or margarine
½ cup honey
¼ cup corn syrup
¼ cup packed brown sugar
2¾ cups uncooked quick oats
⅔ cup raisins
½ cup salted peanuts

Preheat oven to 300°F. Grease 9-inch square baking pan. Melt butter with honey, corn syrup and brown sugar in medium saucepan over medium heat, stirring constantly. Bring to a boil; boil 8 minutes until mixture thickens slightly. Stir in oats, raisins and peanuts until well blended. Press evenly into prepared pan.

Bake 45 to 50 minutes until golden brown. Place pan on wire rack; score top into 2-inch squares. Cool completely. Cut into bars. *Makes 16 bars*

# MOIST PUMPKIN COOKIES

½ cup butter or margarine, softened
1 cup packed brown sugar
½ cup granulated sugar
1½ cups canned pumpkin (not pumpkin pie filling)
1 egg
1 teaspoon vanilla extract
2¼ cups all-purpose flour
1¼ teaspoons ground cinnamon
1 teaspoon baking powder
½ teaspoon baking soda
½ teaspoon salt
½ teaspoon ground nutmeg
¾ cup raisins
½ cup chopped walnuts
Powdered Sugar Glaze (recipe follows)

*(continued)*

Preheat oven to 350°F. Beat butter and sugars in large bowl until creamy. Beat in pumpkin, egg and vanilla until light and fluffy. Mix in flour, cinnamon, baking powder, baking soda, salt and nutmeg until blended. Stir in raisins and walnuts. Drop heaping tablespoonfuls of dough 2 inches apart onto ungreased cookie sheets.

Bake 12 to 15 minutes until set. Cool 2 minutes on cookie sheets. Remove to wire racks; cool completely. Drizzle Powdered Sugar Glaze onto cookies. Let glaze set. Store between layers of waxed paper in airtight containers.

*Makes about 3½ dozen cookies*

***Powdered Sugar Glaze:*** Combine 1 cup powdered sugar and 2 tablespoons milk in small bowl until well blended.

# GINGERBREAD PEOPLE

- ½ cup butter or margarine, softened
- ½ cup packed brown sugar
- ⅓ cup molasses
- ⅓ cup water
- 1 egg
- 4 cups all-purpose flour
- 2 teaspoons baking soda
- 1 teaspoon ground ginger
- ½ teaspoon ground allspice
- ½ teaspoon ground cinnamon
- ½ teaspoon ground cloves
- White or colored decorators frostings

Beat butter and brown sugar in large bowl with electric mixer until creamy. Add molasses, water and egg; beat until blended. Stir in flour, baking soda, ginger, allspice, cinnamon and cloves until well blended. Cover; refrigerate about 2 hours or until firm.

Preheat oven to 350°F. Grease cookie sheets. Roll out dough to ⅛-inch thickness on lightly floured surface with lightly floured rolling pin. Cut with cookie cutter. Place 2 inches apart on prepared cookie sheets.

Bake 12 to 15 minutes until firm to the touch. Cool 1 minute on cookie sheets. Remove to wire racks; cool completely. Decorate with frostings. Store in airtight containers.

*Makes about 4½ dozen cookies*

# HOLIDAY SUGAR COOKIES

  1 cup butter or margarine, softened
¾ cup sugar
  1 egg
  2 cups all-purpose flour
  1 teaspoon baking powder
¼ teaspoon ground cinnamon
¼ teaspoon salt
  Colored sprinkles or sugar, for decorating (optional)

Beat butter and sugar in large bowl with electric mixer until creamy. Add egg; beat until fluffy. Stir in flour, baking powder, cinnamon and salt until well blended. Form into a ball; wrap in plastic wrap and flatten. Refrigerate about 2 hours or until firm.

Preheat oven to 350°F. Roll out dough, a small portion at a time, to ¼-inch thickness on lightly floured surface with lightly floured rolling pin. (Keep remaining dough in refrigerator.) Cut with 3-inch cookie cutter. Sprinkle with colored sprinkles, if desired. Transfer to ungreased cookie sheets.

Bake 7 to 9 minutes until edges are lightly browned. Cool 1 minute on cookie sheets. Remove to wire racks; cool completely. Store in airtight container.

*Makes about 3 dozen cookies*

**Gift Tag Cookies:** Prepare dough as directed; divide into 4 pieces. Shape each piece into a ball; wrap in plastic wrap. Refrigerate 2 hours or up to 3 days. Roll out each ball on lightly floured surface to ¼-inch thickness. (Keep remaining dough in refrigerator.) Cut into gift tag shapes; push drinking straw or skewer into each cookie to make ¼-inch hole. Omit colored sprinkles. Bake as directed. Spread with Buttercream Frosting (page 48) or other white icing. Pipe names and/or decorations with different colored decorators frostings and use red licorice strands as "string" for the tags.

**Sugar Cookie Gift Boxes:** Prepare and roll out dough as directed. Cut dough into squares with a pastry wheel or ravioli cutter. Bake and cool as directed. Stack 4 or 5 cookies; tie with ribbon.

*Left to right: Holiday Sugar Cookies and*
*Gingerbread People (page 43)*

# ELEPHANT EARS

1 package (17¼ ounces) frozen puff pastry, thawed according to
  package directions
1 egg, beaten
¼ cup sugar, divided
2 squares (1 ounce each) semisweet chocolate

Preheat oven to 375°F. Grease cookie sheets; sprinkle lightly with water.
Roll one sheet of pastry to 12×10-inch rectangle. Brush with egg; sprinkle
with 1 tablespoon sugar. Tightly roll up 10-inch sides, meeting in center.
Brush center with egg and seal rolls tightly together; turn over. Cut into
⅜-inch-thick slices. Place slices on prepared cookie sheets. Sprinkle with
1 tablespoon sugar. Repeat with remaining pastry, egg and sugar. Bake
16 to 18 minutes until golden brown. Remove to wire racks; cool completely.

Melt chocolate in small saucepan over low heat, stirring constantly. Remove
from heat. Spread bottoms of cookies with chocolate. Place on wire rack,
chocolate sides up. Let stand until chocolate is set. Store between layers of
waxed paper in airtight containers.          *Makes about 4 dozen cookies*

# CHOCOLATE RASPBERRY THUMBPRINTS

1½ cups butter or margarine, softened
 1 cup sugar
 1 egg
 1 teaspoon vanilla extract
 3 cups all-purpose flour
 ¼ cup unsweetened cocoa
 ½ teaspoon salt
 1 cup (6 ounces) semisweet mini chocolate chips
 ⅔ cup raspberry preserves
   Powdered sugar (optional)

Preheat oven to 350°F. Grease cookie sheets. Beat butter and sugar in large
bowl. Beat in egg and vanilla until light and fluffy. Mix in flour, cocoa and salt
until well blended. Stir in chocolate chips. Roll level tablespoonfuls of dough
into balls. Place 2 inches apart onto prepared cookie sheets. Make deep
indentation in center of each ball with thumb.

Bake 12 to 15 minutes until just set. Cool 2 minutes on cookie sheets. Remove
to wire racks; cool completely. Fill centers with raspberry preserves and
sprinkle with powdered sugar, if desired. Store between layers of waxed
paper in airtight containers.          *Makes about 4½ dozen cookies*

*Elephant Ears (top) and Chocolate*
*Raspberry Thumbprints (bottom)*

# SANTA'S FAVORITE BROWNIES

1 cup (6 ounces) milk chocolate chips
½ cup butter or margarine
¾ cup granulated sugar
2 eggs
1 teaspoon vanilla extract
1¼ cups all-purpose flour
3 tablespoons unsweetened cocoa
1 teaspoon baking powder
½ teaspoon salt
½ cup chopped walnuts
    Buttercream Frosting (recipe follows) *and* jelly beans and
        icing gels, for decoration (optional)

Preheat oven to 350°F. Grease 9-inch square baking pan. Melt chocolate and butter with granulated sugar in medium saucepan over low heat, stirring constantly. Pour into large bowl; add eggs and vanilla. Beat with electric mixer until well blended. Stir in flour, cocoa, baking powder and salt; blend well. Fold in walnuts. Spread into prepared pan.

Bake 25 to 30 minutes until wooden pick inserted in center comes out clean. Place pan on wire rack; cool completely. Frost with Buttercream Frosting, if desired. Cut into squares. Decorate with jelly beans and icing gels, if desired. Store in airtight container. *Makes 16 brownies*

# Buttercream Frosting

3 cups powdered sugar, sifted
½ cup butter or margarine, softened
3 to 4 tablespoons milk, divided
½ teaspoon vanilla extract

Combine powdered sugar, butter, 2 tablespoons milk and vanilla in large bowl. Beat with electric mixer on low speed until blended. Beat on high speed until light and fluffy, adding more milk, 1 teaspoon at a time, as needed for good spreading consistency. *Makes about 1½ cups frosting*

*Santa's Favorite Brownies*

# HONEY SPICE BALLS

½ cup butter or margarine, softened
½ cup packed brown sugar
1 egg
1 tablespoon honey
1 teaspoon vanilla extract
2 cups all-purpose flour
½ teaspoon baking powder
½ teaspoon ground cinnamon
¼ teaspoon ground nutmeg
 Uncooked quick oats

Preheat oven to 350°F. Grease cookie sheets. Beat butter and brown sugar in large bowl with electric mixer until creamy. Add egg, honey and vanilla; beat until light and fluffy. Stir in flour, baking powder, cinnamon and nutmeg until well blended. Shape tablespoonfuls of dough into balls; roll in oats. Place 2 inches apart on prepared cookie sheets.

Bake 15 to 18 minutes until cookie tops crack slightly. Cool 1 minute on cookie sheets. Remove to wire racks; cool completely. Store in airtight container.                                         *Makes about 2½ dozen cookies*

# HOMEMADE COCONUT MACAROONS

3 egg whites
¼ teaspoon cream of tartar
⅛ teaspoon salt
¾ cup sugar
2¼ cups shredded coconut, toasted*
1 teaspoon vanilla extract

Preheat oven to 325°F. Line cookie sheets with parchment paper or foil. Beat egg whites, cream of tartar and salt in large bowl with electric mixer until soft peaks form. Beat in sugar, 1 tablespoon at a time, until egg whites are stiff and shiny. Fold in coconut and vanilla. Drop tablespoonfuls of dough 4 inches apart onto prepared cookie sheets; spread each into 3-inch circle with back of spoon.

Bake 18 to 22 minutes until light brown. Cool 1 minute on cookie sheets. Remove to wire racks; cool completely. Store in airtight container.
                                               *Makes about 2 dozen cookies*

*To toast coconut, spread evenly on cookie sheet. Toast in 350°F oven for 3 minutes. Stir and toast 1 to 2 minutes more until light golden brown.

*Homemade Coconut Macaroons (left) and*
*Honey Spice Balls (right)*

# CINNAMONY APPLE STREUSEL BARS

1¼ cups graham cracker crumbs
1¼ cups all-purpose flour
¾ cup packed brown sugar, divided
¼ cup granulated sugar
1 teaspoon ground cinnamon
¾ cup butter or margarine, melted
2 cups chopped apples (2 medium apples, cored and peeled)
Glaze (recipe follows)

Preheat oven to 350°F. Grease 13×9-inch baking pan. Combine graham cracker crumbs, flour, ½ cup brown sugar, granulated sugar, cinnamon and melted butter in large bowl until well blended; reserve 1 cup. Press remaining crumb mixture into bottom of prepared pan.

Bake 8 minutes. Remove from oven; set aside. Toss apples with remaining ¼ cup brown sugar in medium bowl until brown sugar is dissolved; arrange apples over baked crust. Sprinkle reserved 1 cup crumb mixture over filling. Bake 30 to 35 minutes more until apples are tender. Remove pan to wire rack; cool completely. Drizzle with Glaze. Cut into bars.     *Makes 3 dozen bars*

***Glaze:*** Combine ½ cup powdered sugar and 1 tablespoon milk in small bowl until well blended.

# FRUITCAKE COOKIES

½ cup butter or margarine, softened
¾ cup sugar
1 egg
½ cup milk
2 tablespoons orange juice
1 tablespoon vinegar
2 cups all-purpose flour
1 teaspoon baking powder
½ teaspoon baking soda
¼ teaspoon salt
½ cup chopped walnuts
½ cup chopped candied mixed fruit
½ cup raisins
¼ cup chopped dried pineapple
Powdered sugar

*(continued)*

Preheat oven to 350°F. Grease cookie sheets. Beat butter and sugar in large bowl until creamy. Beat in egg, milk, orange juice and vinegar until blended. Mix in flour, baking powder, baking soda and salt. Stir in walnuts, mixed fruit, raisins and pineapple. Drop rounded tablespoonfuls of dough 2 inches apart onto prepared cookie sheets.

Bake 12 to 14 minutes until lightly browned around edges. Cool 2 minutes on cookie sheets. Remove to wire racks; cool completely. Dust with powdered sugar. Store in airtight container. *Makes about 2½ dozen cookies*

# OLD WORLD PFEFFERNÜSSE COOKIES

½ cup butter or margarine, softened
¾ cup packed brown sugar
½ cup molasses
1 egg
1 tablespoon licorice-flavored liqueur (optional)
3¼ cups all-purpose flour
1 teaspoon baking soda
1 teaspoon ground cinnamon
½ teaspoon ground cloves
¼ teaspoon ground nutmeg
Dash pepper
Powdered sugar

Preheat oven to 350°F. Grease cookie sheets. Beat butter and brown sugar in large bowl until creamy. Beat in molasses, egg and liqueur, if desired, until light and fluffy. Mix in flour, baking soda, cinnamon, cloves, nutmeg and pepper. Shape level tablespoonfuls of dough into balls. Place 2 inches apart onto prepared cookie sheets.

Bake 12 to 14 minutes until set. Cool 2 minutes on cookie sheets. Remove to wire racks; sprinkle with powdered sugar. Cool completely. Store in airtight containers. *Makes about 4 dozen cookies*

# SCOTTISH SHORTBREAD

**5 cups all-purpose flour**
**1 cup rice flour**
**2 cups butter or margarine, softened**
**1 cup sugar**
  **Candied fruit (optional)**

Preheat oven to 325°F. Sift together flours. Beat butter and sugar in large bowl with electric mixer until creamy. Blend in ¾ of flour until mixture resembles fine crumbs. Stir in remaining flour by hand. Press dough firmly into ungreased 15½×10½×1-inch jelly-roll pan *or* two 9-inch fluted tart pans; crimp and flute edges, if desired. Bake 40 to 45 minutes until light brown. Place pan on wire rack. Cut into bars or wedges while warm. Decorate with candied fruit, if desired. Cool completely. Store in airtight containers.

*Makes about 4 dozen bars or 24 wedges*

# ALMOND CRESCENTS

  **1 cup butter or margarine, softened**
  **⅓ cup granulated sugar**
**1¾ cups all-purpose flour**
  **¼ cup cornstarch**
  **1 teaspoon vanilla extract**
**1½ cups ground almonds, toasted***
  **Chocolate Glaze (recipe follows) or powdered sugar**

Preheat oven to 325°F. Beat butter and granulated sugar in large bowl until creamy. Mix in flour, cornstarch and vanilla. Stir in almonds. Shape tablespoonfuls of dough into crescents. Place 2 inches apart on ungreased cookie sheets. Bake 22 to 25 minutes until light brown. Cool 1 minute. Remove to wire racks; cool completely. Drizzle with Chocolate Glaze, if desired. Allow chocolate to set, then store in airtight container. Or, before serving, sprinkle with powdered sugar.     *Makes about 3 dozen cookies*

*Chocolate Glaze:* Place ½ cup semisweet chocolate chips and 1 tablespoon butter or margarine in small resealable plastic bag. Place bag in bowl of hot water for 2 to 3 minutes until chocolate is softened. Dry with paper towel. Knead until chocolate is smooth. Snip pinpoint corner in bag. Drizzle chocolate over cookies.

*To toast almonds, spread on cookie sheet. Bake at 325°F for 4 minutes or until fragrant and golden.

*Scottish Shortbread (top) and*
*Almond Crescents (bottom)*

# LEMONY BUTTER COOKIES

½ cup butter, softened
½ cup sugar
1 egg
1½ cups all-purpose flour
2 tablespoons fresh lemon juice
1 teaspoon grated lemon peel
½ teaspoon baking powder
⅛ teaspoon salt
Additional sugar

Beat butter and ½ cup sugar in large bowl with electric mixer until creamy. Beat in egg until light and fluffy. Mix in flour, lemon juice and peel, baking powder and salt. Cover; refrigerate about 2 hours or until firm.

Preheat oven to 350°F. Roll out dough, a small portion at a time, to ¼-inch thickness on well-floured surface with floured rolling pin. (Keep remaining dough in refrigerator.) Cut with 3-inch round cookie cutter. Transfer to ungreased cookie sheets. Sprinkle with sugar.

Bake 8 to 10 minutes until lightly browned on edges. Cool 1 minute on cookie sheets. Remove to wire racks; cool completely. Store in airtight container.

*Makes about 2½ dozen cookies*

# YULETIDE LINZER BARS

1⅓ cups butter or margarine, softened
¾ cup granulated sugar
1 egg
1 teaspoon lemon peel
2½ cups all-purpose flour
1½ cups whole almonds, ground
1 teaspoon ground cinnamon
¾ cup raspberry preserves
Powdered sugar

Preheat oven to 350°F. Grease 13×9-inch baking pan. Beat butter and granulated sugar in large bowl until creamy. Beat in egg and lemon peel until blended. Mix in flour, almonds and cinnamon until well blended. Press 2 cups flour mixture into bottom of prepared pan. Spread preserves over crust. Press remaining flour mixture, a small amount at a time, evenly over preserves. Bake 35 to 40 minutes until golden brown. Remove pan to wire rack; cool completely. Sprinkle with powdered sugar. Cut into bars.

*Makes 3 dozen bars*

*Lemony Butter Cookies*

## FESTIVE LEBKUCHEN

3 tablespoons butter or margarine
1 cup packed brown sugar
¼ cup honey
1 egg
  Grated peel and juice of 1 lemon
3 cups all-purpose flour
2 teaspoons ground allspice
½ teaspoon baking soda
½ teaspoon salt
  White decorators frosting

Melt butter with brown sugar and honey in medium saucepan over low heat, stirring constantly. Pour into large bowl. Cool 30 minutes. Add egg, lemon peel and juice; beat 2 minutes with electric mixer on high speed. Stir in flour, allspice, baking soda and salt until well blended. Cover; refrigerate overnight or up to 3 days.

Preheat oven to 350°F. Grease cookie sheet. Roll out dough to ½-inch thickness on lightly floured surface with lightly floured rolling pin. Cut with 3-inch cookie cutter. Transfer to prepared cookie sheet. Bake 15 to 18 minutes until edges are light brown. Cool 1 minute. Remove to wire rack; cool completely. Decorate with white frosting. Store in airtight container.

*Makes 1 dozen cookies*

## CHOCOLATE-DIPPED FINGERS

1 cup butter or margarine, softened
½ cup sifted powdered sugar
1¾ cups all-purpose flour
½ teaspoon almond extract
3 squares (1 ounce each) semisweet chocolate, melted
⅓ cup ground almonds

Preheat oven to 350°F. Grease cookie sheets. Beat butter and powdered sugar in large bowl until creamy. Mix in flour and almond extract until well blended. Place ½-inch round or star tip in pastry bag; add dough. Pipe 2½-inch lengths of dough onto prepared cookie sheets.

Bake 13 to 16 minutes until set. Cool 1 minute on cookie sheets. Remove to wire racks; cool completely. Dip one cookie end into chocolate; shake off excess. Sprinkle chocolate end with almonds. Repeat with remaining cookies. Let chocolate set. Store in airtight containers.

*Makes about 4½ dozen cookies*

# LOADED OATMEAL COOKIES

3/4 cup butter or margarine, softened
1 cup packed brown sugar
1 egg
1 tablespoon milk
1 teaspoon vanilla extract
1 1/2 cups uncooked quick oats
1 cup all-purpose flour
1/2 teaspoon baking soda
1/2 teaspoon salt
1/2 teaspoon ground cinnamon
1 cup (6 ounces) semisweet chocolate chips
1 cup (6 ounces) butterscotch chips
3/4 cup raisins
1/2 cup chopped walnuts

Preheat oven to 350°F. Beat butter and brown sugar in large bowl until creamy. Beat in egg, milk and vanilla until light and fluffy. Mix in oats, flour, baking soda, salt and cinnamon until well blended. Stir in chips, raisins and walnuts. Drop rounded tablespoonfuls of dough 2 inches apart onto ungreased cookie sheets.

Bake 12 to 15 minutes until lightly browned around edges. Cool 2 minutes on cookie sheets. Remove to wire racks; cool completely. Store in airtight container. *Makes about 3 dozen cookies*

# ORANGE-CASHEW COOKIES

1/2 cup butter or margarine, softened
2/3 cup sugar
1 egg
1 teaspoon grated orange peel
3 tablespoons orange juice
2 cups all-purpose flour
1 teaspoon baking soda
1/4 teaspoon salt
1 cup chopped cashews

Preheat oven to 350°F. Beat butter and sugar in large bowl until creamy. Beat in egg, orange peel and juice until light and fluffy. Mix in flour, baking soda and salt until well blended. Stir in cashews. Drop tablespoonfuls of dough 2 inches apart onto ungreased cookie sheets.

Bake 9 minutes or until lightly browned. Remove to wire racks; cool completely. Store in airtight container. *Makes about 1 1/2 dozen cookies*

# Holiday Candies

## CHOCOLATE BUTTER CRUNCH

　　1 cup butter or margarine
　1¼ cups sugar
　　¼ cup water
　　2 tablespoons light corn syrup
　　1 cup ground almonds, divided
　　½ teaspoon vanilla extract
　　¾ cup milk chocolate chips

Line 15½ × 10½ × 1-inch jelly-roll pan with foil, extending edges over sides of pan. Generously grease foil and a narrow metal spatula with butter.

Melt butter in 2-quart saucepan over medium heat. Add sugar, water and corn syrup. Bring to a boil, stirring constantly.

Carefully clip candy thermometer to side of pan (do not let bulb touch bottom of pan). Cook until thermometer registers 290°F, stirring frequently. Stir in ⅔ cup almonds and vanilla. Pour into prepared pan. Spread mixture into corners with prepared spatula. Let stand 1 minute. Sprinkle with chocolate chips. Let stand 2 to 3 minutes more until chocolate melts. Spread chocolate over candy. Sprinkle with remaining ⅓ cup almonds. Cool completely.

Lift candy out of pan using foil; remove foil. Break candy into pieces. Store in airtight container. *Makes about 1½ pounds*

*Top to bottom: Mocha Marshmallow Fudge (page 62) and Chocolate Butter Crunch*

# MOCHA MARSHMALLOW FUDGE

   1 tablespoon instant coffee
   1 tablespoon boiling water
2½ cups sugar
   ½ cup butter or margarine
   1 can (5 ounces) evaporated milk (⅔ cup)
1½ cups semisweet chocolate chips
   1 jar (7 ounces) marshmallow creme
   ½ teaspoon vanilla extract

Line 9-inch square baking pan with foil, extending edges over sides of pan. Lightly grease foil with butter. Dissolve coffee in water; set aside.

Place sugar, butter and evaporated milk in 2-quart saucepan; bring to a boil over medium-high heat, stirring constantly. Reduce heat to medium. Continue boiling 5 minutes, stirring constantly. Remove from heat. Immediately stir in reserved coffee mixture, chocolate, marshmallow creme and vanilla. Pour into prepared pan. Let stand 1 hour.

Lift candy out of pan using foil; remove foil. Cut into 1-inch squares. Cover; refrigerate until fudge is set.     *Makes about 2½ pounds or 64 pieces*

# CREAMY CARAMELS

   ½ cup slivered or chopped toasted almonds (optional)
   1 cup butter or margarine, cut into small pieces
   1 can (14 ounces) sweetened condensed milk
   2 cups sugar
   1 cup light corn syrup
1½ teaspoons vanilla extract

Line 8-inch square baking pan with foil, extending edges over sides of pan. Lightly grease foil; sprinkle almonds over bottom of pan, if desired.

Melt butter in heavy 2-quart saucepan over low heat. Add milk, sugar and corn syrup. Stir over low heat until sugar is dissolved and mixture comes to a boil. Carefully clip candy thermometer to side of pan (do not let bulb touch

*(continued)*

bottom of pan). Cook over low heat about 30 minutes or until thermometer registers 240°F (soft-ball stage), stirring occasionally. Immediately remove from heat and stir in vanilla. Pour mixture into prepared pan. Cool completely.

Lift caramels out of pan using foil; remove foil. Place on cutting board; cut into 1-inch squares with sharp knife. Wrap each square in plastic wrap. Store in airtight container.            *Makes about 2½ pounds or 64 caramels*

# EASY ORANGE TRUFFLES

 1 cup (6 ounces) semisweet chocolate chips
 2 squares (1 ounce each) unsweetened chocolate, chopped
 1½ cups powdered sugar
 ½ cup butter or margarine, softened
 1 tablespoon grated orange peel
 1 tablespoon orange-flavored liqueur
 2 squares (1 ounce each) semisweet chocolate, grated *or*
       unsweetened cocoa

Melt chocolate chips and unsweetened chocolate in heavy small saucepan over very low heat, stirring constantly; set aside.

Combine powdered sugar, butter, orange peel and liqueur in small bowl. Beat with electric mixer until combined. Beat in cooled chocolate. Pour into pie pan. Refrigerate about 30 minutes or until mixture is fudgy and can be shaped into balls.

Shape scant 1 tablespoonful of mixture into 1-inch ball. Repeat with remaining mixture. Roll balls in your palms to form uniform round shapes; place on waxed paper.

Sprinkle grated chocolate or cocoa in shallow bowl. Roll balls in grated chocolate or cocoa; place in petit four or candy cases. (If coating mixture won't stick because truffle has set, roll between your palms until outside is soft.) Store in airtight container up to 3 days in refrigerator or several weeks in freezer.            *Makes about 34 truffles*

**Tip:** Truffles are coated with cocoa, powdered sugar, nuts, sprinkles or cookie crumbs to add flavor and prevent the truffle from melting in your fingers.

# MERRI-MINT TRUFFLES

1 package (10 ounces) mint chocolate chips
⅓ cup whipping cream
¼ cup butter or margarine
1 container (3½ ounces) chocolate sprinkles

Melt chocolate chips with cream and butter in heavy medium saucepan over low heat, stirring occasionally. Pour into pie pan. Refrigerate about 2 hours or until mixture is fudgy, but soft.

Shape about 1 tablespoonful of mixture into 1¼-inch ball. Repeat with remaining mixture. Roll balls in your palms to form uniform round shapes; place on waxed paper.

Place sprinkles in shallow bowl. Roll balls in sprinkles; place in petit four or candy cases. (If coating mixture won't stick because truffle has set, roll between your palms until outside is soft.) Store in airtight container up to 3 days in refrigerator or several weeks in freezer.     *Makes about 24 truffles*

# JOLLY BOURBON BALLS

1 package (12 ounces) vanilla wafers, finely crushed (3 cups)
1 cup finely chopped nuts
1 cup powdered sugar, divided
1 cup (6 ounces) semisweet chocolate chips
½ cup light corn syrup
⅓ cup bourbon or rum

Combine crushed wafers, nuts and ½ cup powdered sugar in large bowl; set aside.

Melt chocolate with corn syrup in top of double boiler over simmering (not boiling) water. Stir in bourbon until smooth. Pour chocolate mixture over crumb mixture; stir to combine thoroughly. Shape scant 1 tablespoonful of mixture into 1-inch ball. Repeat with remaining mixture. Roll balls in your palms to form uniform round shapes; place on waxed paper.

Place remaining ½ cup powdered sugar in shallow bowl. Roll balls in powdered sugar; place in petit four or candy cases. Store in airtight containers at least 3 days before serving for flavors to mellow. (May be stored up to 2 weeks.)     *Makes about 48 candies*

*Top box (left to right): Merri-Mint Truffles,*
*Easy Orange Truffles (page 63) and*
*Jolly Bourbon Balls*

# POPCORN CRUNCHIES

  12 **cups popped popcorn (about ¾ cup unpopped)**
1½ **cups sugar**
  ⅓ **cup water**
  ⅓ **cup corn syrup**
   2 **tablespoons butter or margarine**
   1 **teaspoon vanilla extract**

Preheat oven to 250°F. Grease large shallow roasting pan. Add popcorn. Keep warm in oven while making caramel mixture.

Place sugar, water and corn syrup in heavy 2-quart saucepan. Stir over low heat until sugar has dissolved and mixture comes to a boil. Carefully clip candy thermometer to side of pan (do not let bulb touch bottom of pan). Cook over low heat about 10 minutes or until thermometer registers 280°F, without stirring. Occasionally wash down any sugar crystals that form on sides of the pan using pastry brush dipped in warm water. Immediately remove from heat. Stir in butter and vanilla until smooth.

Pour hot syrup mixture slowly over warm popcorn, turning to coat kernels evenly. Set aside until cool enough to handle but warm enough to shape. Butter hands. Working quickly, lightly press warm mixture into 2-inch balls. Cool completely. Store in airtight container.

*Makes about 14 popcorn balls*

**Tips:** If making Popcorn Crunchies to eat, insert lollipop sticks while still warm; set aside to cool completely. Cover with decorative plastic wrap. If making Popcorn Crunchies for tree ornaments, cool balls completely and wrap each ball with enough decorative plastic wrap to pull wrap together at top. Secure with a ribbon which can be formed into a bow or a loop for hanging.

*Popcorn Crunchies*

# CANDIED CITRUS PEEL

    **6 large thick-skinned oranges**
    **5 cups sugar, divided**
**1½ cups water**

Remove peel from white part of oranges in long strips with sharp paring knife. Reserve fruit for another use. Discard all pithy fruit membranes from peel. Cut peel into 2×½-inch strips. (There will be some oddly shaped pieces.) Place sheet of waxed paper under wire rack. Bring 4 cups water to a boil in heavy 3-quart saucepan over high heat. Add peel; return to a boil. Reduce heat to low. Cover; cook 20 minutes. Drain. Repeat boiling process 2 times.

Dissolve 4½ cups sugar in 1½ cups water in same saucepan; bring to a boil over medium heat, stirring occasionally. Reduce heat to low. Carefully clip candy thermometer to side of pan (do not let bulb touch bottom of pan). Cook over low heat about 20 minutes or until thermometer registers 230°F, without stirring. Add drained peel. Cook over low heat about 20 minutes more or until thermometer registers 240°F (soft-ball stage), stirring occasionally. Remove from heat. Remove strips with slotted spoon to wire rack over waxed paper. Discard syrup or save for another use. Cool strips until syrup has dripped off.

Put remaining ½ cup sugar on another sheet of waxed paper. Roll strips, one at a time, in sugar. Set strips on wire rack about 1 hour or until dry. Store in airtight container. Keep in a cool place up to 2 weeks. If strips become slightly sticky, roll again in additional sugar. *Makes about 90 strips*

**Variation:** Melt ½ cup semisweet chocolate chips and 1 tablespoon butter in small saucepan over low heat, stirring until smooth. Dip one end of each strip in melted chocolate; set on wire rack over waxed paper to dry. Let chocolate set completely before storing in airtight container.

# COAL CANDY

    **2 cups sugar**
**¾ cup light corn syrup**
**½ cup water**
    **1 teaspoon anise extract**
**½ teaspoon black paste food coloring**

Line 8-inch square baking pan with foil, extending edges over sides of pan. Lightly grease foil with butter.

*(continued)*

Measure sugar, corn syrup and water into heavy 2-quart saucepan. Stir over medium-low heat until sugar is dissolved and mixture comes to a boil, being careful not to splash sugar mixture on side of pan. Carefully clip candy thermometer to side of pan (do not let bulb touch bottom of pan). Cook about 15 minutes until thermometer registers 290°F, without stirring. Immediately remove from heat. Stir in anise extract and food coloring. Pour mixture into prepared pan. Cool completely.

Lift candy out of pan using foil; remove foil. Place candy between 2 layers of heavy-duty foil. Pound with mallet to break candy into 1- to 2-inch pieces.

*Makes about 1½ pounds*

# CHOCOLATE-DIPPED PEANUT BUTTER CANDIES

**Dipping Chocolate (recipe follows)**
**½ cup creamy peanut butter**
**6 tablespoons butter or margarine, softened**
**1 tablespoon light corn syrup**
**1 teaspoon vanilla extract**
**2 cups powdered sugar**
**1 cup graham cracker crumbs**

Line large cookie sheet with waxed paper. Prepare Dipping Chocolate; keep warm.

Beat peanut butter, butter, corn syrup and vanilla in large bowl with electric mixer on medium speed until smooth, scraping down side of bowl once. Beat in powdered sugar and graham cracker crumbs on low speed until well mixed, scraping down side of bowl once. (Mixture will look dry.)

Shape level tablespoonfuls of peanut butter mixture into balls. Place on prepared cookie sheet. Dip one ball into Dipping Chocolate. Lift coated ball out of chocolate with fork, tapping fork on side of cup to remove excess chocolate. Place on prepared cookie sheet. Repeat with remaining balls. Let chocolate set completely before storing in airtight container.

*Makes about 2½ dozen candies*

***Dipping Chocolate:*** Place 1 cup (6 ounces) semisweet chocolate chips and 2 tablespoons vegetable shortening in 2-cup glass measuring cup. Microwave on HIGH (100%) about 2 minutes or until melted, stirring after 1½ minutes.

# ELEGANT CREAM CHEESE MINTS

Chocolate Topping (recipe follows), optional
1 package (3 ounces) cream cheese, softened
3 tablespoons butter or margarine, softened
½ teaspoon vanilla extract
¼ to ½ teaspoon desired food coloring
¼ teaspoon peppermint extract
1 pound powdered sugar (3½ to 4 cups)
⅓ cup granulated sugar

Line large cookie sheet with waxed paper. Prepare Chocolate Topping, if desired; keep warm.

Beat cream cheese, butter, vanilla, food coloring and peppermint extract in large bowl with electric mixer on medium speed until smooth, scraping side of bowl once. Gradually beat in powdered sugar on low speed until well combined, scraping side of bowl several times. (If necessary stir in remaining powdered sugar with wooden spoon or knead candy on work surface sprinkled lightly with powdered sugar.)

Place granulated sugar in shallow bowl. Roll 2 teaspoons of cream cheese mixture into a ball. Roll ball in granulated sugar until coated. Flatten ball with fingers or fork to make a patty. Place patty on prepared cookie sheet. Repeat with remaining cream cheese mixture and sugar. Drizzle patties with topping, if desired. Refrigerate until firm. Store in airtight container in refrigerator. *Makes about 1½ pounds or 40 (1-inch) mints*

*Chocolate Topping:* Place ½ cup semisweet chocolate chips and 1 tablespoon vegetable shortening in 1-cup glass measuring cup. Microwave on HIGH (100%) about 2 minutes or until melted, stirring after 1½ minutes.

*Top to bottom: Citrus Candied Nuts (page 72)*
*and Elegant Cream Cheese Mints*

# CITRUS CANDIED NUTS

    1 egg white
1½ cups whole almonds
1½ cups pecan halves
    1 cup powdered sugar
    2 tablespoons lemon juice
    2 teaspoons grated orange peel
    1 teaspoon grated lemon peel
⅛ teaspoon ground nutmeg

Preheat oven to 300°F. Generously grease 15½ × 10½ × 1-inch jelly-roll pan. Beat egg white in medium bowl with electric mixer on high speed until soft peaks form. Add almonds and pecans; stir until coated. Stir in powdered sugar, lemon juice, orange peel, lemon peel and nutmeg. Turn out onto prepared pan, spreading nuts in single layer.

Bake 30 minutes, stirring after 20 minutes. *Turn off oven.* Let nuts stand in oven 15 minutes more. Immediately remove nuts from pan to sheet of foil. Cool completely. Store up to 2 weeks in airtight container.

*Makes about 3 cups nuts*


# MRS. CLAUS'S GREAT GRAPE GUMDROPS

1¼ cups sugar, divided
    1 cup light corn syrup
¾ cup grape juice
    1 box (1¾ ounces) powdered fruit pectin
½ teaspoon baking soda
    3 drops blue food coloring

Line 9 × 5-inch loaf pan with foil, extending edges over sides of pan. Lightly grease foil with butter.

Bring 1 cup sugar and corn syrup to a boil in 2-quart saucepan over medium-low heat, stirring constantly. Carefully clip candy thermometer to side of pan (do not let bulb touch bottom of pan). Cook until thermometer registers 280°F, without stirring. Reduce heat to low.

Meanwhile, combine juice, pectin and baking soda in 3-quart saucepan. Bring to a boil over medium heat, stirring constantly. Boil 1 minute. Reduce heat to low; cook until thermometer registers 280°F.

*(continued)*

Slowly pour hot pectin mixture into sugar mixture, stirring occasionally. (This should take about 2 minutes.) Remove from heat; stir in food coloring. Pour into prepared pan. Let stand at room temperature 24 hours.

Lift candy out of pan using foil; remove foil. Cut into squares using knife dipped into sugar. Roll squares in remaining ¼ cup sugar to coat and place on sheet of waxed paper. Let stand at room temperature 1 hour. Store in airtight container.                                          *Makes about 1 pound or 64 gumdrops*

**Mint Gumdrops:** Prepare recipe as directed, substituting ¾ cup water for grape juice and 3 drops green food coloring for blue food coloring. Stir in ½ teaspoon peppermint extract with food coloring.

# DARK CHOCOLATE FUDGE

  ½ **cup whipping cream**
  ½ **cup light corn syrup**
  3 **cups (18 ounces) semisweet chocolate chips**
1½ **cups powdered sugar, sifted**
  ½ **cup chopped walnuts (optional)**
1½ **teaspoons vanilla extract**

Line 8-inch square baking pan with foil, extending edges over sides of pan.

Bring cream and corn syrup to a boil in heavy 2-quart saucepan over medium heat. Boil 1 minute. Remove from heat. Stir in chocolate. Cook until chocolate is melted, stirring constantly. Stir in powdered sugar, walnuts and vanilla. Pour into prepared pan. Spread mixture into corners. Cover; refrigerate 2 hours or until firm.

Lift fudge out of pan using foil; remove foil. Place on cutting board; cut into 1-inch squares. Store in airtight container.
*Makes about 2 pounds or 64 candies*

**Peanut Butter Fudge:** Prepare Dark Chocolate Fudge as directed, substituting 2 packages (10 ounces each) peanut butter chips for the semisweet chocolate chips.                                    *Makes about 2¼ pounds or 64 candies*

# TRADITIONAL PEANUT BRITTLE

1½ cups salted peanuts
1 cup sugar
1 cup light corn syrup
¼ cup water
2 tablespoons butter or margarine
¼ teaspoon baking soda

Heavily butter large cookie sheet. Place peanuts in ungreased 8-inch square baking pan. To warm peanuts, place in oven and heat oven to 250°F.

Meanwhile, place sugar, corn syrup, water and butter in heavy 2-quart saucepan. Stir over medium-low heat until sugar has dissolved and mixture comes to a boil, being careful not to splash sugar mixture on side of pan. Carefully clip candy thermometer to side of (do not let bulb touch bottom of pan). Cook over medium-low heat until thermometer registers 280°F, without stirring. Gradually stir in warm peanuts. Cook until thermometer registers 300°F, stirring frequently.

Immediately remove from the heat; stir in baking soda until thoroughly blended. (Mixture will froth and foam.) Immediately pour onto prepared cookie sheet. Spread mixture evenly to form an even layer. Cool about 30 minutes or until set. Break brittle into pieces. Store in airtight container.

*Makes about 1½ pounds*

**Variation:** Use almonds instead of peanuts and stir in ½ teaspoon almond extract with baking soda.

*Top box: Dark Chocolate Fudge and Peanut Butter Fudge (page 73); Middle box: Traditional Peanut Brittle*

# Festive Cakes & Pies

## COUNTRY PECAN PIE

**Pie pastry for single 9-inch pie crust**
1¼ **cups dark corn syrup**
4 **eggs**
½ **cup packed light brown sugar**
¼ **cup butter or margarine, melted**
2 **teaspoons all-purpose flour**
1½ **teaspoons vanilla extract**
1½ **cups pecan halves**

Preheat oven to 350°F. Roll pastry on lightly floured surface to form 13-inch circle. Fit into 9-inch pie plate. Trim edges; flute. Set aside.

Combine corn syrup, eggs, brown sugar and melted butter in large bowl; beat with electric mixer on medium speed until well blended. Stir in flour and vanilla until blended. Pour into unbaked pie crust. Arrange pecans on top.

Bake 40 to 45 minutes until center of filling is puffed and golden brown. Cool completely on wire rack. Garnish as desired.          *Makes one 9-inch pie*

*Country Pecan Pie*

# CREAMY CHOCOLATE MARBLE
# CHEESECAKE

Cinnamon Graham Crust (recipe follows)
3 packages (8 ounces each) cream cheese, softened
¾ cup sugar
3 eggs
1 cup dairy sour cream
1 teaspoon vanilla extract
1 square (1 ounce) unsweetened chocolate, melted

Prepare Cinnamon Graham Crust.

Preheat oven to 450°F. Beat cream cheese in large bowl with electric mixer on medium speed until fluffy. Beat in sugar on medium speed until light and fluffy. Beat in eggs, 1 at a time, on low speed until well blended. Stir in sour cream and vanilla on low speed. Blend melted chocolate into 1 cup batter. Spoon plain and chocolate batters alternately over crust. Cut through batters several times with a knife for marble effect.

Bake 10 minutes. *Reduce oven temperature to 250°F.* Bake 30 minutes more or until center is just set. Remove pan to wire rack. Carefully loosen edge of cake with narrow knife. Cool completely on wire rack. Refrigerate several hours or overnight.

To serve, place on plate. Carefully remove side of pan.

*Makes one 9-inch cheesecake*

**Variation:** For plain cheesecake, omit melted chocolate. Proceed as directed.

## Cinnamon Graham Crust

1 cup graham cracker crumbs
3 tablespoons sugar
½ teaspoon ground cinnamon
3 tablespoons butter or margarine, melted

Preheat oven to 350°F. Combine crumbs, sugar and cinnamon in small bowl. Stir in melted butter until blended. Press onto bottom of 9-inch springform pan. Bake 10 minutes. Cool on wire rack while preparing filling.

*Top to bottom: Cheesecake (variation) and*
*Creamy Chocolate Marble Cheesecake*

# APPLE-TOPPED MAPLE CREAM TART

Nut Pastry Crust (recipe follows)
1½ cups light cream or half-and-half
¾ cup pure maple syrup, divided
2 tablespoons granulated sugar
2 tablespoons cornstarch
6 egg yolks
1 teaspoon vanilla extract
1 large green tart cooking apple, cored and thinly sliced
Additional pure maple syrup

Prepare Nut Pastry Crust. Set aside.

Combine cream and ½ cup maple syrup in glass 4-cup measure. Microwave on HIGH (100%) 4 minutes, stirring after 2 minutes. Combine granulated sugar and cornstarch in small bowl. Place egg yolks in medium bowl. Whisk sugar mixture into egg yolks. Whisk about half the hot cream mixture into egg yolks. Return all to 4-cup measure. Microwave on HIGH 2 minutes. Whisk vigorously. Microwave on HIGH 1 minute. Whisk in vanilla. Press cream mixture through fine sieve into clean bowl. Cover with plastic wrap and refrigerate.

Place remaining ¼ cup maple syrup in medium skillet. Heat over medium heat. Stir in sliced apple. Cook and stir slices 3 to 4 minutes until soft but not mushy. Drain apple slices. Spoon maple cream into Nut Pastry Crust. Arrange apples spoke-fashion on top of maple cream. Refrigerate tart 1 to 2 hours. To serve, drizzle additional maple syrup over tart slices.

*Makes one 10-inch tart*

# Nut Pastry Crust

1 cup plus 2 tablespoons all-purpose flour
¼ cup packed light brown sugar
¼ cup finely ground walnuts
½ cup butter or margarine, cut into 8 pieces
1 egg, beaten
2 teaspoons vanilla extract

Combine flour, brown sugar and walnuts in food processor bowl or blender; cover. Process until combined. Add butter; process until coarse crumbs are formed. Add egg and vanilla; process until stiff dough is formed. Wrap in plastic wrap; refrigerate 1 to 2 hours.

Preheat oven to 375°F. Roll dough on lightly floured surface to form 13-inch circle. Fit into 10-inch tart pan with removable bottom. Trim edges. Prick bottom and sides of dough with fork. Bake 18 to 20 minutes until golden. Remove pan to wire rack; cool completely.

# PECAN SPICE CAKE WITH BROWNED BUTTER FROSTING

    1 package (18 to 19 ounces) moist yellow cake mix
    ¾ cup dairy sour cream
    ¾ cup water
    3 eggs
    1 tablespoon grated lemon peel
 1½ teaspoons ground cinnamon
    ½ teaspoon ground nutmeg
    ¼ teaspoon ground allspice
    1 cup chopped pecans
      Browned Butter Frosting (recipe follows)
      Additional chopped pecans (optional)

Preheat oven to 350°F. Grease two 9-inch square baking pans. Combine cake mix, sour cream, water, eggs, lemon peel and spices in large bowl with electric mixer on low speed until ingredients are moistened. Beat on high speed 2 minutes, scraping sides of bowl frequently. Stir in 1 cup pecans. Divide evenly into prepared pans.

Bake 25 to 30 minutes until wooden pick inserted in center comes out clean. Cool in pans 10 minutes. Remove from pans to wire racks; cool completely.

Place one layer on serving plate. Spread with ⅓ of frosting. Top with second layer. Frost sides and top of cake with remaining frosting. Garnish with additional pecans, if desired. Store tightly covered at room temperature.

*Makes 12 to 16 servings*

## Browned Butter Frosting

    ¾ cup butter
 5½ cups sifted powdered sugar
 1½ teaspoons vanilla extract
      Dash salt
    8 to 9 tablespoons light cream or half-and-half

Heat butter in heavy 1-quart saucepan over medium heat until butter is melted and light amber in color, stirring frequently. Cool butter slightly. Combine browned butter, powdered sugar, vanilla, salt and 8 tablespoons cream in large bowl. Beat on medium speed until smooth and of spreading consistency. Stir in 1 tablespoon cream if frosting is too stiff.

# CHOCOLATE CREAM-FILLED CAKE ROLL

¾ **cup sifted cake flour**
¼ **cup unsweetened cocoa**
½ **teaspoon baking powder**
¼ **teaspoon salt**
4 **eggs**
¾ **cup granulated sugar**
1 **tablespoon water**
1 **teaspoon vanilla extract**
  **Powdered sugar**
  **Cream Filling (recipe page 84)**
  **Chocolate Stars (recipe page 84)**
  **Sweetened whipped cream**
  **Fresh raspberries and mint leaves, for garnish (optional)**

Preheat oven to 375°F. Grease bottom of 15½ × 10½ × 1-inch jelly-roll pan. Line with waxed paper. Grease paper and sides of pan; dust with flour. Combine flour, cocoa, baking powder and salt in small bowl; set aside. Beat eggs in medium bowl with electric mixer on high speed about 5 minutes or until thick and lemon colored. Add granulated sugar, a little at a time, beating well on medium speed; beat until thick and fluffy. Stir in water and vanilla. Fold in flour mixture on low speed until smooth. Spread evenly in prepared pan.

Bake 12 to 15 minutes until wooden pick inserted in center comes out clean. Meanwhile, sprinkle towel with powdered sugar. Loosen cake edges and turn out onto prepared towel. Carefully peel off waxed paper. Roll up cake with towel inside, starting with narrow end. Cool, seam side down, 20 minutes on wire rack.

Meanwhile, prepare Cream Filling and Chocolate Stars. Unroll cake and spread with Cream Filling. Roll up again, without towel. Cover and refrigerate at least 1 hour before serving. Dust with additional powdered sugar before serving. Place star tip in pastry bag; add sweetened whipped cream. Pipe rosettes on top of cake. Place points of Chocolate Stars into rosettes. Garnish with raspberries and mint, if desired. Store tightly covered in refrigerator.

*Makes 8 to 10 servings*

*(continued)*

*Chocolate Cream-Filled Cake Roll*

## Cream Filling

1 teaspoon unflavored gelatin
¼ cup cold water
1 cup whipping cream
2 tablespoons powdered sugar
1 tablespoon orange-flavored liqueur

Sprinkle gelatin over cold water in small saucepan; let stand 1 minute to soften. Heat over low heat until dissolved, stirring constantly. Cool to room temperature. Beat cream, powdered sugar and liqueur in small chilled bowl with electric mixer on high speed until stiff peaks form. Fold in gelatin mixture on low speed. Cover and refrigerate 5 to 10 minutes.

## Chocolate Stars

Melt 2 squares (1 ounce each) semisweet chocolate in heavy small saucepan over low heat, stirring frequently. Pour onto waxed-paper-lined cookie sheet. Spread to ⅛-inch thickness with small metal spatula. Refrigerate about 15 minutes or until firm. Cut out stars with cookie cutter. Carefully lift stars from waxed paper using metal spatula or knife. Refrigerate until ready to use.

## SPICY PUMPKIN PIE

Pie pastry for single 9-inch pie crust
1 can (16 ounces) pumpkin (not pumpkin pie filling)
¾ cup packed light brown sugar
2 teaspoons ground cinnamon
¾ teaspoon ground ginger
½ teaspoon ground nutmeg
¼ teaspoon salt
⅛ teaspoon ground cloves
4 eggs, slightly beaten
1½ cups light cream or half-and-half
1 teaspoon vanilla extract
Sweetened whipped cream

Preheat oven to 400°F. Roll pie pastry on lightly floured surface to form 13-inch circle. Fit into 9-inch pie plate. Trim edges; flute. Set aside.

*(continued)*

Combine pumpkin and brown sugar in large bowl; mix well. Stir in cinnamon, ginger, nutmeg, salt and cloves. Add eggs; mix well. Gradually stir in cream and vanilla, mixing until combined. Pour pumpkin mixture into unbaked pie crust.

Bake 40 to 45 minutes until knife inserted near center comes out clean. Cool on wire rack. Serve warm topped with sweetened whipped cream.

*Makes one 9-inch pie*

# RUM AND SPUMONI LAYERED TORTE

> 1 package (18 to 19 ounces) moist butter yellow cake mix
> 3 eggs
> ½ cup butter or margarine, softened
> ⅓ cup plus 2 teaspoons rum, divided
> ⅓ cup water
> 1 quart spumoni ice cream, softened
> 1 cup whipping cream
> 1 tablespoon powdered sugar
> Chopped mixed candied fruit
> Red and green sugar, for decorating (optional)

Preheat oven to 375°F. Grease and flour 15½ × 10½ × 1-inch jelly-roll pan. Combine cake mix, eggs, butter, ⅓ cup rum and water in large bowl. Beat with electric mixer on low speed until moistened. Beat on high speed for 4 minutes. Pour evenly into prepared pan.

Bake 20 to 25 minutes until wooden pick inserted in center comes out clean. Cool in pan 10 minutes. Turn out of pan onto wire rack; cool completely.

Cut cake into three 10 × 5-inch pieces. Place one cake layer on serving plate. Spread with half the softened ice cream. Cover with second cake layer. Spread with remaining ice cream. Place remaining cake layer on top. Gently push down. Wrap cake in plastic wrap and freeze at least 4 hours.

Just before serving, combine cream, powdered sugar and remaining 2 teaspoons rum in small chilled bowl. Beat on high speed with chilled beaters until stiff peaks form. Remove cake from freezer. Spread thin layer of whipped cream mixture over *top* of cake. Place star tip in pastry bag; add remaining whipped cream mixture. Pipe rosettes around outer top edges of cake. Place candied fruit in narrow strip down center of cake. Sprinkle colored sugar over rosettes, if desired. Serve immediately.

*Makes 8 to 10 servings*

# CRANBERRY APPLE NUT PIE

Rich Pie Pastry (recipe follows)
1 cup sugar
3 tablespoons all-purpose flour
¼ teaspoon salt
4 cups sliced peeled tart apples (4 large)
2 cups fresh cranberries
½ cup golden raisins
½ cup coarsely chopped pecans
1 tablespoon grated lemon peel
2 tablespoons butter or margarine
1 egg, beaten

Preheat oven to 425°F. Divide dough in half. Roll half of pie pastry on lightly floured surface to form 13-inch circle. Fit into 9-inch pie plate; trim edges. Reroll scraps and cut into decorative shapes, such as holly leaves and berries, for garnish; set aside.

Combine sugar, flour and salt in large bowl. Stir in apples, cranberries, raisins, pecans and lemon peel; toss well. Spoon fruit mixture into unbaked pie crust. Dot with butter. Roll remaining half of pie pastry on lightly floured surface to form 11-inch circle. Place over filling. Trim and seal edges; flute. Cut 3 slits in center of top crust. Moisten pastry cutouts and decorate as desired. Lightly brush top crust with egg.

Bake 35 to 40 minutes until apples are tender when pierced with a fork and pastry is golden brown. Cool in pan on wire rack. Serve warm or cool completely.

*Makes one 9-inch pie*

# Rich Pie Pastry

2 cups all-purpose flour
¼ teaspoon salt
6 tablespoons butter
6 tablespoons lard
6 to 8 tablespoons cold water

Combine flour and salt in medium bowl. Cut in butter and lard with pastry blender or 2 knives until mixture resembles coarse crumbs. Sprinkle water, 1 tablespoon at a time, over flour mixture, mixing until flour is moistened. Shape dough into a ball. Roll, fill and bake as recipe directs.

*Makes pastry for one 9-inch double pie crust*

**Note:** For single crust, cut recipe in half.

*Cranberry Apple Nut Pie*

# GLAZED APPLESAUCE SPICE CAKE

¾ cup butter or margarine
1 cup packed light brown sugar
3 eggs
1½ teaspoons vanilla extract
2¼ cups all-purpose flour
2 teaspoons baking soda
2 teaspoons ground cinnamon
¾ teaspoon ground nutmeg
½ teaspoon ground ginger
¼ teaspoon salt
1½ cups unsweetened applesauce
½ cup milk
⅔ cup chopped walnuts
⅔ cup butterscotch chips
Apple Glaze (recipe follows)

Preheat oven to 350°F. Grease and lightly flour 12-cup Bundt pan or 10-inch tube pan. Beat butter in large bowl with electric mixer on medium speed until creamy. Beat in brown sugar until light and fluffy. Beat in eggs and vanilla until well blended. Combine flour, baking soda, cinnamon, nutmeg, ginger and salt. Add flour mixture to butter mixture on low speed, alternately with applesauce and milk, beginning and ending with flour mixture. Beat well after each addition. Stir in walnuts and butterscotch chips. Spoon into prepared pan.

Bake 45 to 50 minutes until wooden pick inserted in center comes out clean. Cool in pan 15 minutes. Remove from pan to wire rack; cool completely. Spoon Apple Glaze over top of cake. Store tightly covered at room temperature.                                   *Makes one 10-inch round cake*

***Apple Glaze:*** Place 1 cup sifted powdered sugar in small bowl. Whisk in 2 to 3 tablespoons apple juice concentrate to form stiff glaze.

# TRIPLE CHOCOLATE PEPPERMINT CHEESECAKE

    **Chocolate Crumb Crust (recipe follows)**
 **1 cup mint semisweet chocolate chips**
 **1 cup (6 ounces) semisweet chocolate chips**
 **¾ cup whipping cream**
 **3 packages (8 ounces each) cream cheese, softened**
 **¾ cup packed brown sugar**
 **3 eggs**
 **¼ cup unsweetened cocoa**
 **1 teaspoon vanilla extract**
    **Sweetened whipped cream, for garnish**
    **Crushed peppermint candy, for garnish**

Preheat oven to 325°F. Prepare Chocolate Crumb Crust; set aside.

Melt chocolates with cream in heavy small saucepan over low heat, stirring until smooth; set aside. Beat cream cheese in large bowl with electric mixer on medium speed until fluffy. Beat in brown sugar until light and fluffy. Beat in eggs, 1 at a time, on low speed until well blended. Stir in cocoa and vanilla. Blend chocolate mixture into cream cheese mixture on low speed, scraping side of bowl frequently. Spoon into prepared crust.

Bake 45 to 50 minutes until center of cake is just set. Remove pan to wire rack. Carefully loosen edge of cake with narrow knife. Cool completely on wire rack. Refrigerate several hours or overnight.

To serve, place on plate. Carefully remove side of pan. Place star tip in pastry bag; add sweetened whipped cream. Pipe rosettes on outside edge of cake. Sprinkle rosettes with crushed peppermint candy.

*Makes one 9-inch cheesecake*

*Chocolate Crumb Crust:* Preheat oven to 325°F. Combine 1 cup chocolate wafer crumbs and 3 tablespoons melted butter or margarine in small bowl until well blended. Press onto bottom only of 9-inch springform pan. Bake 10 minutes. Cool on wire rack while preparing filling.

# GOLDEN HOLIDAY FRUITCAKE

1½ cups butter or margarine, softened
1½ cups sugar
6 eggs
2 teaspoons grated lemon peel
2 tablespoons fresh lemon juice
3 cups all-purpose flour
2 teaspoons baking powder
½ teaspoon baking soda
¼ teaspoon salt
1½ cups golden raisins
1½ cups pecan halves
1½ cups red and green candied pineapple chunks
1 cup dried apricot halves, cut in half
1 cup halved red candied cherries
1 cup halved green candied cherries
Light corn syrup
Candied fruit and nuts, for garnish

Preheat oven to 325°F. Grease and flour 10-inch tube pan. Beat butter in large bowl with electric mixer on medium speed until creamy. Add sugar; beat until light and fluffy. Add eggs, 1 at a time, beating well after each addition. Stir in lemon peel and juice. Combine flour, baking powder, baking soda and salt in large bowl. Reserve ½ cup flour mixture. Gradually blend remaining flour mixture into butter mixture on low speed. Combine raisins, pecans, pineapple, apricots and cherries in large bowl. Toss fruit mixture with reserved ½ cup flour mixture. Stir fruit mixture into butter mixture. Spoon evenly into prepared pan.

Bake 80 to 90 minutes until wooden pick inserted in center comes out clean. Cool in pan 15 minutes. Remove from pan to wire rack; cool completely. Store up to 1 month tightly covered at room temperature. (If desired, cake may be stored wrapped in a wine- or brandy-soaked cloth in airtight container. Cake may be frozen up to 2 months.)

Before serving, lightly brush surface of cake with corn syrup. Arrange candied fruit and nuts decoratively on top. Brush with corn syrup.

*Makes one 10-inch round fruitcake*

*Golden Holiday Fruitcake*

# TRIPLE CHOCOLATE CAKE

¾ cup butter or margarine, softened
1½ cups sugar
1 egg
1 teaspoon vanilla extract
2 cups all-purpose flour
⅔ cup unsweetened cocoa
2 teaspoons baking soda
¼ teaspoon salt
1 cup buttermilk
¾ cup dairy sour cream
Light Ganache Filling (recipe follows)
Dark Chocolate Glaze (recipe follows)

Preheat oven to 350°F. Grease and flour two 9-inch round cake pans. Beat butter and sugar in large bowl with electric mixer on medium speed until light and fluffy. Beat in egg and vanilla until blended. Combine flour, cocoa, baking soda and salt in medium bowl. Add flour mixture to butter mixture, alternately with buttermilk and sour cream, beginning and ending with flour mixture. Beat well after each addition. Divide evenly into cake pans.

Bake 30 to 35 minutes until wooden pick inserted in center comes out clean. Cool in pans 10 minutes. Remove from pans to wire racks; cool completely.

Meanwhile, prepare Light Ganache Filling. Place one cake layer on serving plate. Spread with Light Ganache Filling. Top with second cake layer. Prepare Dark Chocolate Glaze. Pour over top of cake. Immediately spread glaze over sides and top with spatula until smooth. Refrigerate cake at least 30 minutes to set glaze. Garnish as desired. Store tightly covered at room temperature.

*Makes one 9-inch layer cake*

# Light Ganache Filling

4 squares (1 ounce each) semisweet chocolate
1 cup whipping cream
½ teaspoon vanilla extract

Melt chocolate in heavy small saucepan over low heat, stirring frequently. Pour melted chocolate into small bowl. Wash and dry saucepan. Heat cream in same saucepan over medium heat until hot; *do not boil*. Gradually whisk cream into chocolate. Whisk in vanilla. Let filling stand at room temperature until of spreading consistency. Beat mixture with electric mixer on high until light and fluffy.

*(continued)*

## Dark Chocolate Glaze

**8 squares (1 ounce each) semisweet chocolate**
**4 tablespoons butter or margarine**
**1 cup whipping cream**

Melt chocolate and butter in heavy small saucepan over low heat, stirring frequently. Pour melted chocolate into medium bowl. Wash and dry saucepan. Heat cream in same saucepan over medium heat until hot; *do not boil.* Gradually whisk cream into chocolate mixture until slightly thickened.

# FESTIVE MINCEMEAT TARTLETS

**Pastry for double pie crust**
**1½ cups prepared mincemeat**
**½ cup chopped peeled, cored tart apple**
**⅓ cup golden raisins**
**⅓ cup chopped walnuts**
**3 tablespoons brandy or apple juice concentrate**
**1 tablespoon grated lemon peel**

Preheat oven to 400°F. Divide pastry in half. Refrigerate one half. Roll remaining half on lightly floured surface to form 13-inch circle. Cut six 4-inch rounds. Fit each pastry round into 2¾-inch muffin cup. Prick inside of crust with fork; set aside. Repeat with remaining pastry.

Bake unfilled pastry crusts 8 minutes. Meanwhile, combine mincemeat, apple, raisins, walnuts, brandy and lemon peel in medium bowl until well blended. Remove crusts from oven; fill each with rounded tablespoonful of mincemeat mixture. Press lightly into crust with back of spoon.

Bake 18 to 20 minutes more until crust edges are golden. Cool in pan 5 minutes. Carefully remove from pan to wire rack. Serve warm or cool completely.                                    *Makes twelve 2¾-inch tartlets*

# Index